A

is for Ammon

Book of Mormon Verses

By
Albert R. Lyman and Alberta Lyman O'Brien

Illustrations By
Steven J. Van Wagenen

ISBN: 979-8-9900022-1-012

Rooftop Publishing
Sandy, Utah

Second Printing

Printed in the United States of America

A

is for Ammon

Book of Mormon Verses

A is for Ammon

the son of a king,

expert with his sword

and the use of his sling.

– Alma 17

B

is King Benjamin

who spoke with great power.

He taught all to serve

as he stood on a tower.

– Mosiah 2

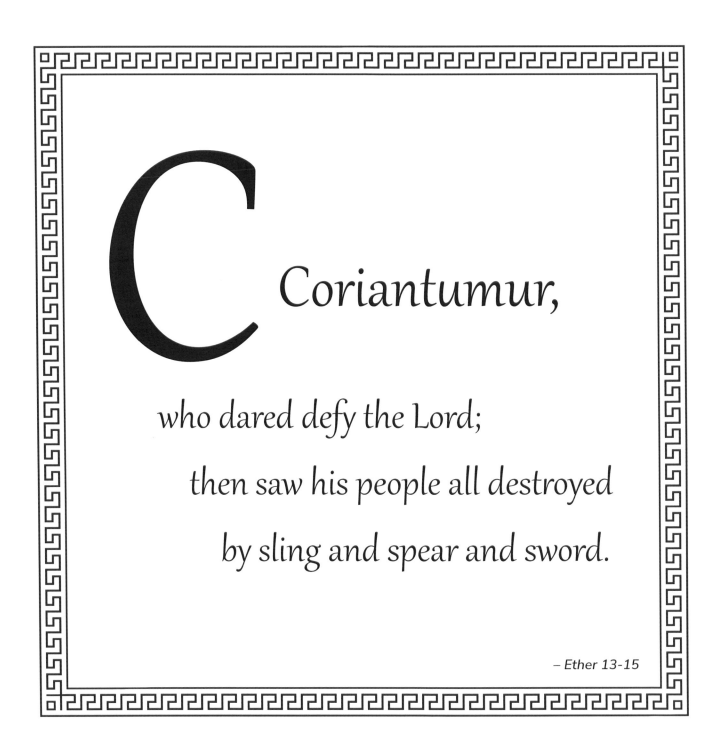

C Coriantumur,

who dared defy the Lord;

then saw his people all destroyed

by sling and spear and sword.

– Ether 13-15

D is for Director

a compass found one day;

a strange and curious ball of brass

designed to point the way.

– 1 Nephi 16

E is for Enos

who went out among the trees,

and spent all day and then the night

in prayer upon his knees.

– Enos 1

F

is for famine.

The Lord withheld all rain

until the people sought the Lord

and turned to Him again.

– Helaman 11

G

is for Gideon,

a strong and righteous man.

Many gained their freedom

through his bold and clever plan.

– Mosiah 22

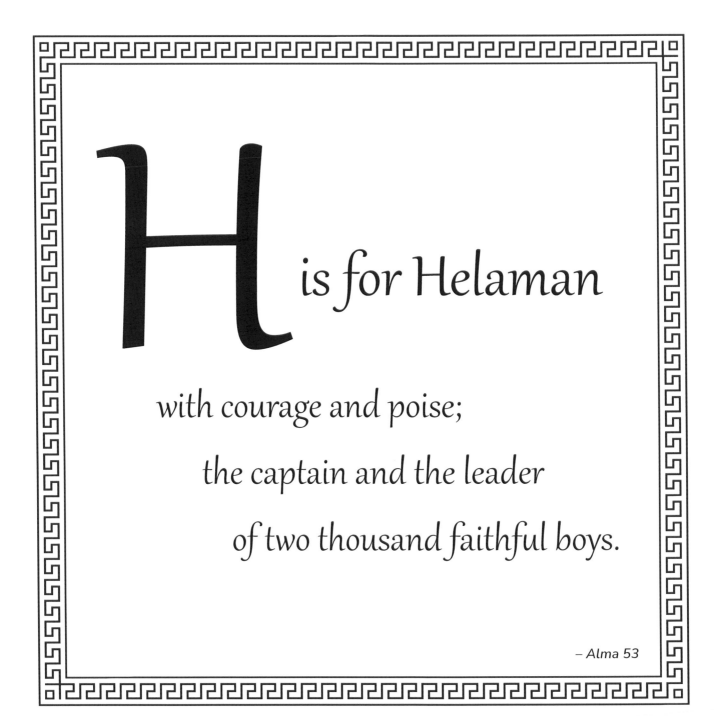

H is for Helaman

with courage and poise;

the captain and the leader

of two thousand faithful boys.

– Alma 53

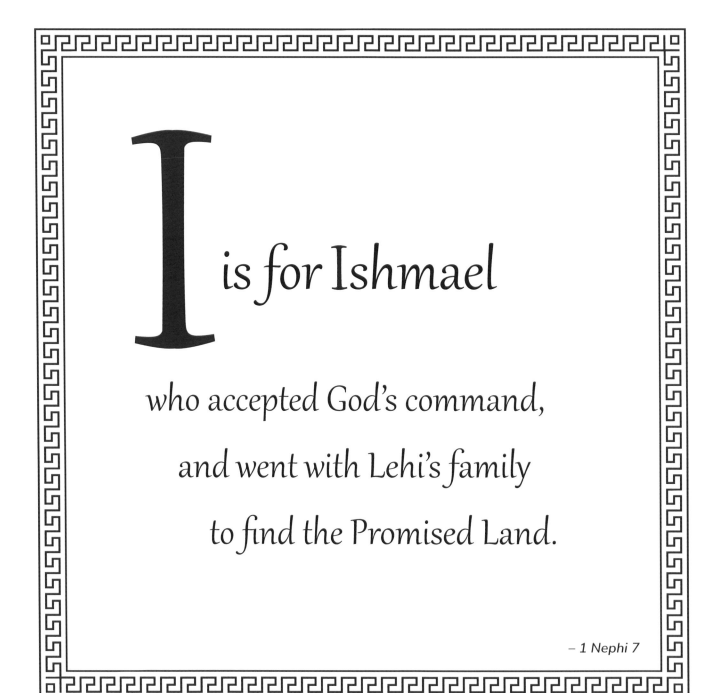

I is for Ishmael

who accepted God's command,
and went with Lehi's family
to find the Promised Land.

– 1 Nephi 7

J

is for Jaredites

who traveled with their band
in barges to live in the
new Promised Land.

– Ether 1

K

is for Korihor,

daring to come

in defiance of truth

'til the Lord struck him dumb.

– Alma 30

L is Lord Jesus,

our Savior, King of Kings!

The Book of Mormon testifies

of truths His Gospel brings.

– 3 Nephi 11

M is for Mormon

of warrior-prophet fame.

The most correctly-written book of

scripture bears his sacred name.

– Mormon 1

N is King Noah

the tyrant of shame,

who burned as a rag

in the heat of the flame.

– Mosiah 19

O is Orihah.

As the plates make it known,

he was first to be king

on the Jaredite throne.

– Ether 6

P is Pahoran

righteous judge of the land,

who was stabbed by a thief

with a knife in his hand.

– Helaman 1

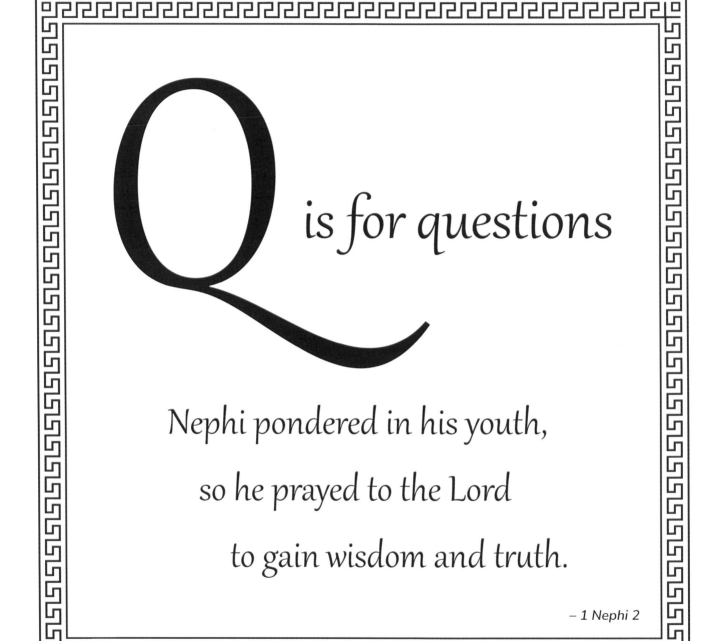

Q is for questions

Nephi pondered in his youth,

so he prayed to the Lord

to gain wisdom and truth.

– 1 Nephi 2

R

is for robbers

who covered the land.

Gadianton was leader

of that wild, wicked band.

– Helaman 2

S

is for Samuel,

whom the Nephites despised.

He withstood their abuse

and of Christ prophesied.

– Helaman 13-14

T

is Teancum

who crept in the dark,

and cast a sharp javelin

straight to its mark.

– Alma 51

U is for upheavel.

At the time of Christ's death

the wicked were punished

'till their very last breath.

– 3 Nephi 8

V is for Vision.

Lehi saw the Iron Rod.

He was told it leads to safety,

for it is the Word of God.

– 1 Nephi 8

W is for wine

shared with drunken guards that night,

and while they slept soundly

the Nephites took flight.

– Mosiah 22

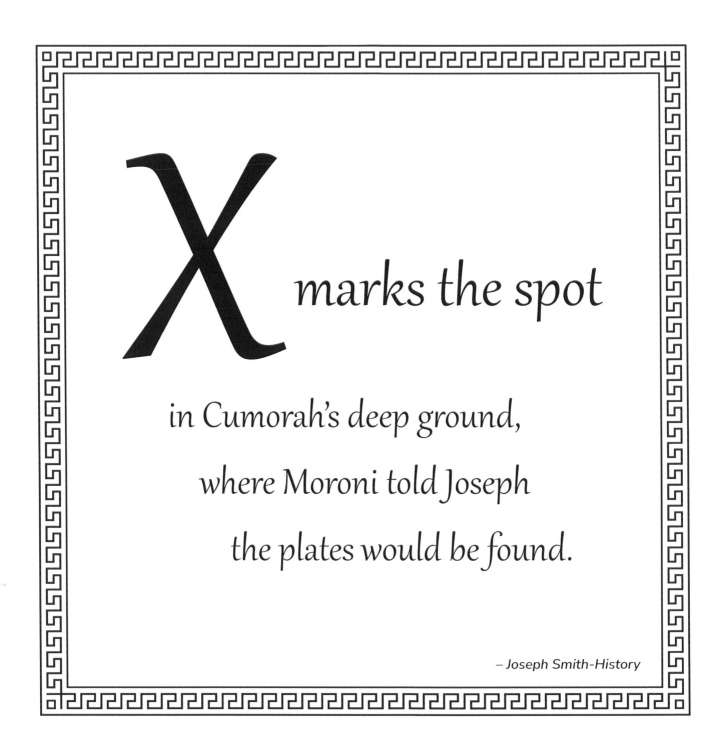

X marks the spot

in Cumorah's deep ground,

where Moroni told Joseph

the plates would be found.

– Joseph Smith-History

Y is for yoke

of sad bondage and pain,

by which Nephites were bound

with the Lamanite chain.

– Mosiah 19

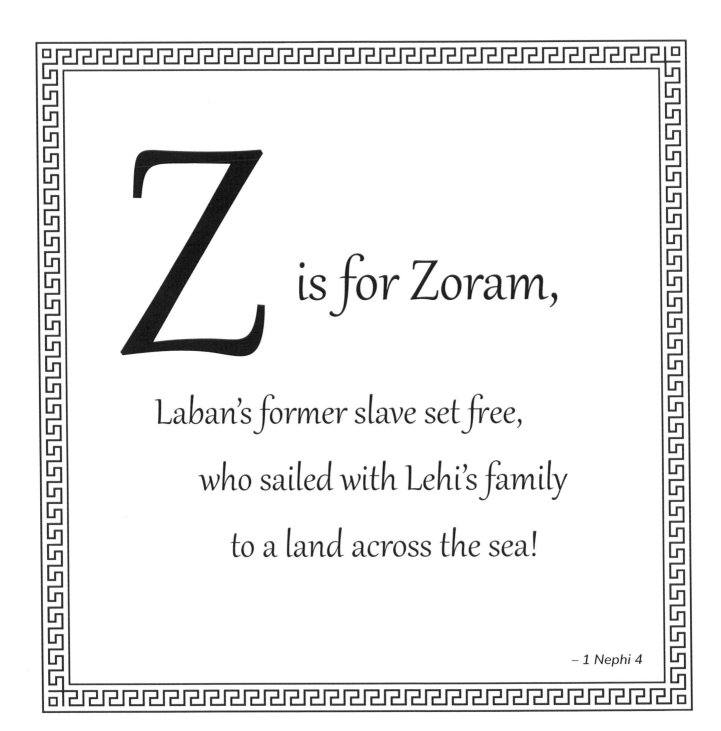

Z is for Zoram,

Laban's former slave set free,

who sailed with Lehi's family

to a land across the sea!

– 1 Nephi 4

Note to Readers

This book is a combination of many talents and a legacy of love.

We are foremost indebted to our grandfather, Albert R. Lyman, whose work has resonated through several generations. He was a prolific writer of our pioneer roots and faith, as well as a devoted father of 15. Keeping journal entries from his early pioneer days, he preserved the sometimes-tragic and heart-wrenching history of southeastern Utah. In addition to his many historical volumes, he was always willing to share his knowledge of the scriptures and his testimony of the Savior. At his daughter's request to write a set of Book of Mormon verses for her children, he sat at her kitchen table, pulled out his stubby pencil and in a short time had completed the project.

Our mother, Alberta Lyman O'Brien, was no less a gifted writer, and many years after receiving this first set of verses, she had a desire to write her own. Bedtime stories and family home evenings in the O'Brien home were taken from scripture as she and our father nurtured and taught their eight children the gospel. It was always her desire to publish the verses, but unfortunately, she never found someone whose artwork she felt was worthy of the sacred nature of the project.

Albert R. Lyman
1880-1973

Alberta Lyman O'Brien
1923-2001

In 2024, two of her daughters, inspired by the desire to teach their growing posterity the family scripture verses, were introduced to an illustrator who captured the feelings and emotions they felt as young children. This book is a collection of verses, some from each set, which they hope will resonate in the hearts and homes where scriptures are cherished.

We extend our appreciation to Steven Van Wagenen, whose illustrations bring the Book of Mormon stories to life.

Many thanks to the team at Rooftop Publishing who contributed their expert help in editing, designing and printing.